Primordial Strength Basketball EPE Volume 1

By Steven Helmicki

ISBN 978-0-557-34566-3

Initial Testing: Vertical Jump_______

Broad Jump________

8 measured vertical jumps averaged________

5 seconds rest between attempts.

8 measured broad jumps averaged_________

5 seconds rest between attempts

10 yard dash________

This is ten week programming to maximize your explosive power and quickness on the court, while improving the vertical jump and first two steps. Train hard.

Train three times per week.

Phase Bsktbll 1- 2 weeks

Warm-up 3 minutes of jump roping

Pre-habilitation- bent arm pullovers x 20 reps, shoulder internal/external rotation with band, knee tracking/glute activation 12 inch box x 6 reps

Workout 1

Vertical box jumps 50% max vertical x 12 singles with 5lb dumbbells 7 seconds rest

Hydration/30 seconds rest

Barbell squat close stance empty bar x 2 reps maximum velocity x 12 sets 7 seconds rest

Hydration/45 seconds rest

4kg kettlebell swings x 15 reps maximum velocity

Hydration/45 seconds rest

8kg kettlebell swings x 15 reps maximum velocity

Stretch

Warm-up 3 minutes of jump roping

Pre-habilitation- bent arm pullovers x 20 reps, shoulder internal/external rotation with band, knee tracking/glute activation 12 inch box x 6 reps

Workout 2

Vertical box jumps 10% max vertical x 7 jumps with 15lb dumbbells

Hydration/45 seconds rest

Kettlebell sumo deadlifts 4kg x 3 immediately followed by 6kg x 3 immediately followed by 8kg x 3 repeat 3 times non-stop maximum velocity

Hydration/ 45 seconds rest

Landmine press 15 lbs x 3 reps x 5 sets 7 seconds rest

Hydration/ 45 seconds rest

Landmine twist empty bar 15 reps maximum velocity

Hydration/ 45 seconds rest

stretch

Warm-up 3 minutes of jump roping

Pre-habilitation- bent arm pullovers x 20 reps, shoulder internal/external rotation with band, knee tracking/glute activation 12 inch box x 6 reps

Workout 3

Broad jumps with 2lb dumbbells x 6 jumps 5 seconds rest

Hydration/ 45 seconds rest

Light band attached to waist x 2 step sprint starts x 6 times 8 seconds rest

Hydration/ 45 seconds rest

Biceps curls x 20 reps

Triceps pushdowns x 20 reps

15lb dumbbell shrugs x 25 reps

Phase Bsktbll 2- 2 weeks

Warm-up 3 minutes of jump roping

Pre-habilitation- bent arm pullovers x 20 reps, shoulder internal/external rotation with band, knee tracking/glute activation 12 inch box x 6 reps

Workout 1

Vertical box jumps with 65% of vertical max with 8lb dumbbells x 6 reps 5 seconds rest

Hydration/30 seconds rest

Empty bar squats x 2 immediately followed by empty bar squat jumps x 2 repeat 3 times non-stop

Hydration/ 45 seconds rest

Kettlebell bent rows 4kg x 3 immediately followed by 8kg x 3 repeat 4 times non-stop

Hydration/ 35 seconds rest

Kettlebell high pulls 4kg x 3 immediately followed by 8kg x 3 repeat 4 times non-stop

Hydration/ 40 seconds rest

Kettlebell swings 4kg x 5 immediately followed by 8kg x 5 repeat 4 times non-stop

Warm-up 3 minutes of jump roping

Pre-habilitation- bent arm pullovers x 20 reps, shoulder internal/external rotation with band, knee tracking/glute activation 12 inch box x 6 reps

Workout 2

Soft landing jumps with 20lb dumbbells (no box) 10 jumps 4 seconds rest

Hydration/ 1 minute rest

65lb barbell squat x 3 reps x 5 sets 10 seconds rest

Hydration/1.5 minutes rest

4kg kettlebell cleans and presses 3 reps x 12 sets 12 seconds rest

Hydration/ 1.5 minutes rest

Double kettlebell swings 4kg x 15 reps

stretch

Warm-up 3 minutes of jump roping

Pre-habilitation- bent arm pullovers x 20 reps, shoulder internal/external rotation with band, knee tracking/glute activation 12 inch box x 6 reps

Workout 3

25 yards of consecutive broad jumps

Hydration/1 minute rest

5 yard dash x 6 times 5 seconds rest

Hydration

10 yard dash x 6 times 5 seconds rest

Hydration/1 minute rest

Kettlebell curls 4kg x 3 immediately followed by 6kg x 3 repeat 3 times non-stop

Hydration

Medicine ball smashes 2kg x 3 immediately followed by 4kg x 3 repeat 4 times non-stop

stretch

Phase Bsktbll 3- 3 weeks

Warm-up 3 minutes of jump roping

Pre-habilitation- bent arm pullovers x 20 reps, shoulder internal/external rotation with band, knee tracking/glute activation 12 inch box x 6 reps

Workout 1

12 inch vertical box jump with 12lb dumbbells immediately followed by 70lb squat repeat 4 times non-stop

Hydration/ 1 minute rest

Landmine press empty bar x 3 immediately followed by bar plus 15lbs x 3 repeat 3 times non-stop

Hydration/I minute rest

Kettlebell snatches 4kg x 2 immediately followed by 6kg x 2 repeat 5 times non-stop

Hydration/ 2 minute rest

Kettlebell swings 4kg x 1 immediately followed by 6kg x 1 immediately followed by 8kg x 1 repeat 6 times non-stop

stretch

Warm-up 3 minutes of jump roping

Pre-habilitation- bent arm pullovers x 20 reps, shoulder internal/external rotation with band, knee tracking/glute activation 12 inch box x 6 reps

Workout 2

6 inch box jump with 10 lb dumbbells x 2 immediately followed by 12 inch box jumps with 5lb dumbbells repeat 3 times non-stop

Hydration/ 1 minute rest

Empty bar squat x 20 reps maximum speed

Hydration/ 1.5 minutes rest

Kettlebell clean and jerks 4kg x 1 immediately followed by 6kg x 1 immediately followed by 8kg x 1 repeat 3 times non-stop

Hydration/ 2 minutes rest

Landmine twists empty bar x 5 immediately followed by bar plus 10lbs x 5 repeat 2 times non-stop

stretch

Warm-up 3 minutes of jump roping

Pre-habilitation- bent arm pullovers x 20 reps, shoulder internal/external rotation with band, knee tracking/glute activation 12 inch box x 6 reps

Workout 3

Bodyweight broad jump x 1 immediately followed by broad jump with 5 lb dumbbells x 4 times non-stop

Hydration/ 2 minutes rest

Two step band starts light x 2 immediately followed by average x 2 repeat 3 times non-stop

Hydration/ 2 minutes rest

10 yard dash x 15 attempts 15 seconds rest

stretch

Phase bsktbll 4- 3 weeks

Warm-up 3 minutes of jump roping

Pre-habilitation- bent arm pullovers x 20 reps, shoulder internal/external rotation with band, knee tracking/glute activation 12 inch box x 6 reps

Workout 1

Empty bar squat x 2 immediately followed by 65lb squat x 2 repeat 4 times non-stop

Hydration/ 1.5 minutes rest

Kettlebell bent rows 6kg x 4 immediately followed by 8kg x 4 repeat 4 times non-stop

Hydration/ 2 minutes rest

Kettlebell shrugs 6kg x 4 immediately followed by 12kg x 4 repeat 4 times non-stop

Hydration/ 1minute rest

Kettlebell curls 4kg x 2 immediately followed by 6 kg x 2 repeat 3 times non-stop

Hydration/ I minute rest

4 kg kettlebell swings x 20 reps

stretch

Warm-up 3 minutes of jump roping

Pre-habilitation- bent arm pullovers x 20 reps, shoulder internal/external rotation with band, knee tracking/glute activation 12 inch box x 6 reps

Workout 2

8 inch box jump bodyweight immediately followed by 12 inch box jump bodyweight immediately followed by 16 inch box jump bodyweight repeat 3 times non-stop

Hydration/ 30 seconds rest

Kettlebell sumo deadlifts 4kg x 2 immediately followed by 12kg x 2 repeat 3 times non-stop

Hydration/ 45 seconds rest

Triceps pushdowns 20lbs x 5 immediately followed by 40lbs x 5 repeat 4 times non-stop

stretch

Warm-up 3 minutes of jump roping

Pre-habilitation- bent arm pullovers x 20 reps, shoulder internal/external rotation with band, knee tracking/glute activation 12 inch box x 6 reps

Workout 3

Broad jump with 15lb dumbbells x 1 immediately followed by 10lb dumbbells x 1 immediately followed by 5lb dumbbells x 1 repeat 2 times non-stop

Hydration/ 1 minute rest

5yard dash x 1 immediately followed by 10 yard dash x 1 repeat 5 times non-stop

Hydration

Kettlebell swings 4kg x 5 immediately followed by 8kg x 5 repeat 2 times

stretch

Phase Bsktbll 5- 2 weeks

Warm-up 3 minutes of jump roping

Pre-habilitation- bent arm pullovers x 20 reps, shoulder internal/external rotation with band, knee tracking/glute activation 12 inch box x 6 reps

Workout 1

12 inch box jump with 5lb dumbbell immediately followed by empty bar squat immediately followed by 16 inch box jump immediately followed by 65lb squat repeat 4 times non-stop

Hydration/ 2 minutes rest

Medicine ball 4kg wall throw immediately followed by empty bar double landmine press repeat 4 times non-stop

Hydration/ 1 minute rest

Landmine twist bar x 5 immediately followed by bar plus 10lbs x 5 immediately followed by bar plus 20lbs x 5 repeat 2 times non-stop

stretch

Warm-up 3 minutes of jump roping

Pre-habilitation- bent arm pullovers x 20 reps, shoulder internal/external rotation with band, knee tracking/glute activation 12 inch box x 6 reps

Workout 2

Mini-band broad jump immediately followed by light band broad jump immediately followed by average band repeat 3 times non-stop

Hydration/ 1 minute rest

15 yard dash x 6 10 seconds rest

Hydration

4kg kettlebell curls x 25 reps

4kg triceps extension x 25 reps

stretch

Warm-up 3 minutes of jump roping

Pre-habilitation- bent arm pullovers x 20 reps, shoulder internal/external rotation with band, knee tracking/glute activation 12 inch box x 6 reps

Workout 3

6kg kettlebell front squat position fascia stretch 15 seconds in the hole immediately followed by 8kg kettlebell front box squat repeat 8 times non-stop

Hydration

Kettlebell swings 4kg x 3 immediately followed by 8kg x 3 immediately followed by 12kg x 3 repeat 4 times non-stop

Hydration

Stride reaches two steps x 5 attempts increasing each attempt by 6 inches. Starting point should be average two step sprint distance

stretch

Phase Bsktbll 6- 1 week

Warm-up 3 minutes of jump roping

Pre-habilitation- bent arm pullovers x 20 reps, shoulder internal/external rotation with band, knee tracking/glute activation 12 inch box x 6 reps

Workout 1

Empty bar speed squats 1 rep x 8 sets 3 seconds rest

Empty bar double landmine press x 1 rep x 8 sets 5 seconds rest

4kg kettlebell swing 1 rep x 8 sets 5 seconds rest

Stretch

Warm-up 3 minutes of jump roping

Pre-habilitation- bent arm pullovers x 20 reps, shoulder internal/external rotation with band, knee tracking/glute activation 12 inch box x 6 reps

Workout 2

Dynamic stretching

Warm-up 3 minutes of jump roping

Pre-habilitation- bent arm pullovers x 20 reps, shoulder internal/external rotation with band, knee tracking/glute activation 12 inch box x 6 reps

Workout 3

Re-test

PRIMORD

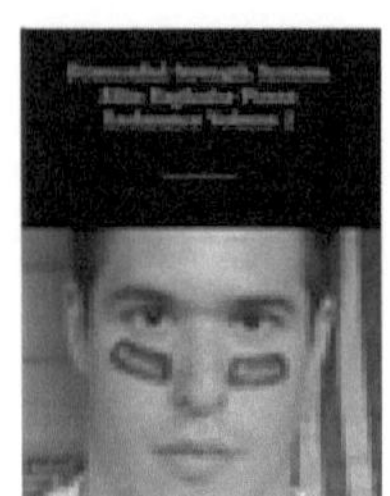

Performance
on the field
Matters Most.

PRIMORDIAL
STRENGTH SYSTEMS

RIMO
STRENGT

TRAIN TO WIN.

TRAIN
TO
WIN

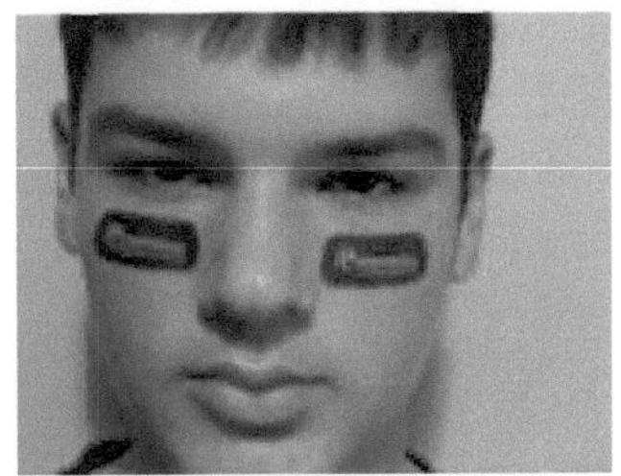

ST FRANCIS

Built to Work. Period.

www.ingramcontent.com/pod-product-compliance
Ingram Content Group UK Ltd.
Pitfield, Milton Keynes, MK11 3LW, UK
UKHW041901190726
13854UKWH00003B/1020